Tertullian

On Fasting

Tertullian

On Fasting

Tertullian
On Fasting

Published by
Lighthouse Christian Publishing
SAN 257-4330
5531 Dufferin Drive
Savage, Minnesota, 55378
United States of America

www.lighthousechristianpublishing.com

Tertullian

On Fasting.

In Opposition to the Psychics.

Chapter I.—Connection of Gluttony and Lust. Grounds of Psychical Objections Against the Montanists.

I should wonder at the Psychics, if they were enthralled to voluptuousness alone, which leads them to repeated marriages, if they were not likewise bursting with gluttony, which leads them to hate fasts. Lust without voracity would certainly be considered a monstrous phenomenon; since these two are so united and concrete, that, had there been any possibility of disjoining them, the pudenda would not have been affixed to the belly itself rather than elsewhere. Look at the body: the region (of these members) is one and the same. In short, the order of the vices is proportionate to the arrangement of the members. First, the belly; and then immediately the materials of all other species of lasciviousness are laid subordinately to daintiness: through love of eating, love of impurity finds passage. I recognize, therefore, *animal* faith by its care of the flesh (of which it wholly consists)—as prone to manifold feeding as to manifold marrying—so that it deservedly accuses the *spiritual* discipline, which according to its ability opposes it, in this species of continence as well; imposing, as it does, reins upon the appetite, through taking, sometimes no meals, or late meals, or dry meals, just as upon lust, through allowing but one marriage.

It is really irksome to engage with such: one is really ashamed to wrangle about subjects the very defense of which is offensive to modesty. For how am I to protect chastity and sobriety without taxing their adversaries? What those adversaries are I will once for all mention: they are the exterior and interior *botuli* of the Psychics. It is these which raise controversy with the Paraclete; it is on this account that the New Prophecies are rejected: not that Montanus and Priscilla and Maximilla preach another God, nor that they disjoin Jesus Christ (from God), nor that they overturn any particular rule of faith or hope, but that they plainly teach more frequent fasting than marrying. Concerning the limit of marrying, we have already published a defense of monogamy. Now our battle is the battle of the secondary (or rather the primary) continence, in regard of the chastisement of diet. They charge us with keeping fasts of our own; with prolonging our Stations generally into the evening; with observing xerophagies likewise, keeping our food unmoistened by any flesh, and by any juiciness, and by any kind of especially succulent fruit; and with not eating or drinking anything with a winey flavor; also with abstinence from the bath, congruent with our dry diet. They are therefore constantly reproaching us with novelty; concerning the unlawfulness of which they lay down a prescriptive rule, that either it must be adjudged *heresy*, if (the point in dispute) is a human presumption; or else pronounced *pseudoprophecy*, if it is a spiritual declaration; provided that, either way, we who reclaim hear (sentence of) anathema.

Chapter II. —Arguments of the Psychics, Drawn from the Law, the Gospel, the Acts, the Epistles, and Heathenish Practices.

For, so far as pertains to fasts, they oppose to us the definite days appointed by God: as when, in Leviticus, the Lord enjoins upon Moses the tenth day of the seventh month (as) a day of atonement, saying, "Holy shall be to you the day, and ye shall vex your souls; and every soul which shall not have been vexed in that day shall be exterminated from his people." At all events, in the Gospel they think that those days were definitely appointed for fasts in which "the Bridegroom was taken away;" and that these are now the only legitimate days for Christian fasts, the legal and prophetical antiquities having been abolished: for wherever it suits their wishes, they recognize what is the meaning of "the Law and the prophets until John." Accordingly, (they think) that, with regard to the future, fasting was to be indifferently observed, by the New Discipline, of choice, not of command, according to the times and needs of each individual: that this, withal, had been the observance of the apostles, imposing (as they did) no other yoke of definite fasts to be observed by all generally, nor similarly of Stations either, which (they think) have withal days of their own (the fourth and sixth days of the week), but yet take a wide range according to individual judgment, neither subject to the law of a given precept, nor (to be protracted) beyond the last hour of the day, since even prayers the ninth hour generally concludes, after Peter's example, which is recorded in the Acts. Xerophagies, however, (they consider) the novel name of a studied duty, and very much akin to heathenish superstition, like the abstemious rigors which purify an Apis, an Isis, and a Magna Mater, by a restriction laid upon certain kinds of food; whereas faith, free in Christ, owes no abstinence from particular meats to the Jewish Law even, admitted as it has been by the apostle once for all to the whole range of the meat market— (the apostle, I say), that detester of such as, in like manner as they prohibit marrying, so bid us abstain from meats created by God. And accordingly (they think) *us* to have been even then prenoted as "in the latest times departing from the faith, giving heed to spirits which seduce the world, having a conscience inburnt with doctrines of liars." (Inburnt?) With what fires, prithee? The fires, I ween, which lead us to repeated contracting of nuptials and daily cooking of dinners! Thus, too, they affirm that we share with the Galatians the piercing rebuke (of the apostle), as "observers of days, and of months, and of years." Meantime they huff in our teeth the fact that Isaiah withal has authoritatively declared, "Not such a fast hath the Lord elected," that is, not abstinence from food, but the works of righteousness, which he there appends: and that the Lord Himself in the Gospel has given a compendious answer to every kind of scrupulousness in regard to food; "that not by such things as are introduced into the mouth is a man defiled, but by such as are produced out of the mouth;" while Himself withal was wont to eat and drink till He made Himself noted thus; "Behold, a gormandizer and a drinker:" (finally), that so, too, does the apostle teach that "food commendeth us not to God; since we neither abound if we eat, nor lack if we eat not."

By the instrumentalities of these and similar passages, they subtlety tend at last to such a point, that everyone who is somewhat prone to appetite finds it possible to regard as superfluous, and not so very necessary, the duties of abstinence from, or diminution or delay of, food, since "God," forsooth, "prefers the works of justice and of innocence." And we know the quality of the hortatory addresses of carnal conveniences, how easy it is to say, "I must believe with my whole heart; I must love God, and my neighbor as myself: for 'on these two precepts the whole Law hangeth, and the prophets,' not on the emptiness of my lungs and intestines."

Chapter III. —The Principle of Fasting Traced Back to Its Earliest Source.

Accordingly, we are bound to affirm, before proceeding further, this (principle), which is in danger of being secretly subverted; (namely), of what value in the sight of God this "emptiness" you speak of is: and, first of all, whence has proceeded the rationale itself of earning the favor of God in this way. For the necessity of the observance will then be acknowledged, when the authority of a rationale, to be dated back from the very beginning, shall have shone out to view.

Adam had received from God the law of not tasting "of the tree of recognition of good and evil," with the doom of death to ensue upon tasting. However, even (Adam) himself at that time, reverting to the condition of a Psychic after the spiritual ecstasy in which he had prophetically interpreted that "great sacrament" with reference to Christ and the Church, and no longer being "capable of the things which were the Spirit's," yielded more readily to his belly than to God, heeded the meat rather than the mandate, and sold salvation for his gullet! He ate, in short, and perished; saved (as he would) else (have been), if he had preferred to fast from one little tree: so that, even from this early date, *animal faith* may recognize its own seed, deducing from thence onward its appetite for carnalities and rejection of spiritualties. I hold, therefore, that from the very beginning the murderous gullet was to be punished with the torments and penalties of hunger. Even if God had enjoined no preceptive fasts, still, by pointing out the source whence Adam was slain, He who had demonstrated the offence had left to my intelligence the remedies for the offence. Unbidden, I would, in such ways and at such times as I might have been able, have habitually accounted food as poison, and taken the antidote, hunger; through which to purge the primordial cause of death—a cause transmitted to me also, concurrently with my very generation; certain that God willed that whereof He nilled the contrary, and confident enough that the care of continence will be pleasing to Him by whom I should have understood that the crime of *in*continence had been condemned. Further: since He Himself both commands fasting, and calls "a soul wholly shattered"—properly, of course, by straits of diet— "a sacrifice;" who will any longer doubt that of all dietary macerations the rationale has been this, that by a renewed interdiction of food and observation of precept the primordial sin might now be expiated, in order that man may make God satisfaction through the self-same causative material through which he had offended, that is, through interdiction of food; and thus, in emulous wise, hunger might rekindle, just as satiety had extinguished, salvation, contemning for the sake of one unlawful more lawful (gratifications)?

Chapter IV. —The Objection is Raised, Why, Then, Was the Limit of Lawful Food Extended After the Flood? The Answer to It.

This rationale was constantly kept in the eye of the providence of God—modulating all things, as He does, to suit the exigencies of the times—lest any from the opposite side, with the view of demolishing our proposition, should say: "Why, in that case, did not God forthwith institute some definite restriction upon food? nay, rather, why did He withal enlarge His permission? For, at the beginning indeed, it had only been the food of herbs and trees which He had assigned to man: 'Behold, I have given you all grass fit for sowing, seeding seed, which is upon the earth; and every tree which hath in itself the fruit of seed fit for sowing shall be to you for food.' Afterwards, however, after enumerating to Noah the subjection (to him) of 'all beasts of the earth, and fowls of the heaven, and things moving on earth, and the fish of the sea, and every creeping thing,' He says, 'They shall be to you for food: just like grassy vegetables have I given (them) you universally: but flesh in the blood of its own soul shall ye not eat.' For even by this very fact, that He exempts from eating that flesh only the 'soul' of which is not out-shed through 'blood,' it is manifest that He has conceded the use of all other flesh." To this we reply, that it was not suitable for man to be burdened with any further special law of abstinence, who so recently showed himself unable to tolerate so light an interdiction—of one single fruit, to wit; that, accordingly, having had the rein relaxed, he was to be strengthened by his very liberty; that equally after the deluge, in the *re*formation of the human race, (as before it), *one* law—of abstaining from blood—was sufficient, the use of all things else being allowed. For the Lord had already shown His judgment through the deluge; had, moreover, likewise issued a comminatory warning through the "requisition of blood from the hand of a brother, and from the hand of every beast." And thus, preministering the justice of judgment, He issued the materials of liberty; preparing through allowance an undergrowth of discipline; permitting all things, with a view to take some away; meaning to "exact more" if He had "committed more;" to command abstinence since He had foresent indulgence: in order that (as we have said) the primordial sin might be the more expiated by the operation of a greater abstinence in the (midst of the) opportunity of a greater license.

Chapter V.—Proceeding to the History of Israel, Tertullian Shows that Appetite Was as Conspicuous Among Their Sins as in Adam's Case. Therefore, the Restraints of the Levitical Law Were Imposed.

At length, when a familiar people began to be chosen by God to Himself, and the restoration of man was able to be essayed, then all the laws and disciplines were imposed, even such as curtailed food; certain things being prohibited as unclean, in order that man, by observing a perpetual abstinence in certain particulars, might at last the more easily tolerate absolute fasts. For the first People had withal reproduced the first man's crime, being found more prone to their belly than to God, when, plucked out from the harshness of Egyptian servitude "by the mighty hand and sublime arm" of God, they were seen to be its lord, destined to the "land flowing with milk and honey;" but forthwith, stumbled at the surrounding spectacle of an incopious desert sighing after the lost enjoyments of Egyptian satiety, they murmured against Moses and Aaron: "Would that we had been smitten to the heart by the Lord, and perished in the land of Egypt, when we were wont to sit over our jars of flesh and eat bread unto the full! How leddest thou us out into these deserts, to kill this assembly by famine?" From the self-same belly preference were they destined (at last) to deplore (the fate of) the self-same leaden of their own and eye-witnesses of (the power of) God, whom, by their regretful hankering after flesh, and their recollection of their Egyptian plenties, they were ever exacerbating: "Who shall feed us with flesh? here have come into our mind the fish which in Egypt we were wont to eat freely, and the cucumbers, and the melons, and the leeks, and the onions, and the garlic. But now our soul is arid: naught save manna do our eyes see!" Thus used they, too, (like the Psychics), to find the angelic bread of xerophagy displeasing: they preferred the fragrance of garlic and onion to that of heaven. And therefore from men so ungrateful all that was more pleasing and appetizing was withdrawn, for the sake at once of punishing gluttony and exercising continence, that the former might be condemned, the latter practically learned.

Chapter VI. —The Physical Tendencies of Fasting and Feeding Considered. The Cases of Moses and Elijah.

Now, if there has been temerity in our retracing to primordial experiences the reasons for God's having laid, and our duty (for the sake of God) to lay, restrictions upon food, let us consult common conscience. Nature herself will plainly tell with what qualities she is ever wont to find us endowed when she sets us, *before* taking food and drink, with our saliva still in a virgin state, to the transaction of matters, by the sense especially whereby things divine are handled; whether (it be not) with a mind much more vigorous, with a heart much more alive, than when that whole habitation of our interior man, stuffed with meats, inundated with wines, fermenting for the purpose of excremental secretion, is already being turned into a premeditatory of privies, (a premeditatory) where, plainly, nothing is so proximately super sequent as the savoring of lasciviousness. "The people did eat and drink, and they arose to play." Understand the modest language of Holy Scripture: "play," unless it had been immodest, it would not have reprehended. On the other hand, how many are there who are mindful of religion, when the seats of the memory are occupied, the limbs of wisdom impeded? No one will suitably, fitly, usefully, remember God at that time when it is customary for a man to forget his own self. All discipline food either slays or else wounds. I am a liar, if the Lord Himself, when upbraiding Israel with forgetfulness, does not impute the cause to "fullness:" "(My) beloved is waxen thick, and fat, and distent, and hath quite forsaken God, who made him, and hath gone away from the Lord his Savior." In short, in the self-same Deuteronomy, when bidding precaution to be taken against the self-same cause, He says: "Lest, when thou shalt have eaten, and drunken, and built excellent houses, thy sheep and oxen being multiplied, and (thy) silver and gold, thy heart be elated, and thou be forgetful of the Lord thy God." To the corrupting power of riches, He made the enormity of edacity antecedent, for which riches themselves are the procuring agents. Through them, to wit, had "the heart of the People been made thick, lest they should see with the eyes, and hear with the ears, and understand with a heart" obstructed by the "fats" of which He had expressly forbidden the eating, teaching man not to be studious of the stomach.

On the other hand, he whose "heart" was habitually found "lifted up" rather than fattened up, who in forty days and as many nights maintained a fast above the power of human nature, while spiritual faith subministered strength (to his body), both saw with his eyes God's glory, and heard with his ears God's voice, and understood with his heart God's law: while He taught him even then (by experience) that man liveth not upon bread alone, but upon every word of God; in that the People, though fatter than he, could not constantly contemplate even Moses himself, fed as he had been upon God, nor his leanness, sated as it had been with His glory! Deservedly, therefore, even while in the flesh, did the Lord show Himself to him, the colleague of His own fasts, no less than to Elijah.

For Elijah withal had, by this fact primarily, that he had imprecated a famine, already sufficiently devoted himself to fasts: "The Lord liveth," he said, "before whom I am standing in His sight, if there shall be dew in these years, and rain-shower." Subsequently, fleeing from threatening Jezebel, after one single (meal of) food and drink, which he had found on being awakened by an angel, he too himself, in a space of forty days and nights, his belly empty, his mouth dry, arrived at Mount Horeb; where, when he had made a cave his inn, with how familiar a meeting with God was he received! "What (doest) thou, Elijah, here?" Much more friendly was this voice than, "Adam, where art thou?" For the latter voice was uttering a threat to a fed man, the former soothing a fasting one. Such is the prerogative of circumscribed food, that it makes God tent-fellow with man—peer, in truth, with peer! For if the eternal God will not hunger, as He testifies through Isaiah, this will be the time for man to be made equal with God, when he lives without food.

Chapter VII. —Further Examples from the Old Testament in Favor of Fasting.

And thus we have already proceeded to examples, in order that, by its profitable efficacy, we may unfold the powers of this duty which reconciles God, even when angered, to man.

Israel, before their gathering together by Samuel on occasion of the drawing of water at Mizpeh, had sinned; but so immediately do they wash away the sin by a fast, that the peril of battle is dispersed by them simultaneously (with the water on the ground). At the very moment when Samuel was offering the holocaust (in no way do we learn that the clemency of God was more procured than by the *abstinence* of the people), and the aliens were advancing to battle, then and there "the Lord thundered with a mighty voice upon the aliens, and they were thrown into confusion, and fell in a mass in the sight of Israel; and the men of Israel went forth out of Mizpeh, and pursued the aliens, and smote them unto Bethor,"—the unfed (chasing) the fed, the unarmed the armed. Such will be the strength of them who "fast to God." For such, Heaven fights. You have (before you) a condition upon which (divine) defense will be granted, necessary even to spiritual wars.

Similarly, when the king of the Assyrians, Sennacherib, after already taking several cities, was volleying blasphemies and menaces against Israel through Rabshakeh, nothing else (but fasting) diverted him from his purpose, and sent him into the Ethiopias. After that, what else swept away by the hand of the angel a hundred eighty and four thousand from his army than Hezekiah the king's humiliation? if it is true, (as it is), that on hearing the announcement of the harshness of the foe, he rent his garment, put on sackcloth, and bade the elders of the priests, similarly habited, approach God through Isaiah—fasting being, of course, the escorting attendant of their prayers. For peril has no time for food, nor sackcloth any care for satiety's refinements. Hunger is ever the attendant of mourning, just as gladness is an accessory of fullness.

Through this attendant of mourning, and (this) hunger, even that sinful state, Nineveh, is freed from the predicted ruin. For repentance for sins had sufficiently commended the fast, keeping it up in a space of three days, starving out even the cattle with which God was not angry. Sodom also, and Gomorrah, would have escaped if they had fasted. This remedy even Ahab acknowledges. When, after his transgression and idolatry, and the slaughter of Naboth, slain by Jezebel on account of his vineyard, Elijah had upbraided him, "How hast thou killed, and possessed the inheritance? In the place where dogs had licked up the blood of Naboth, thine also shall they lick up,"—he "abandoned himself, and put sackcloth upon his flesh, and fasted, and slept in sackcloth. And then (came) the word of the Lord unto Elijah, Thou hast seen how Ahab hath shrunk in awe from my face: for that he hath shrunk in awe I will not bring the hurt upon (him) in his own days; but in the days of his son I will bring it upon (him)"— (his son), who was not to fast. Thus a God-ward fast is a work of reverential awe: and by its means also Hannah the wife of Elkanah making suit, barren as she had been before time, easily obtained from God the filling of her belly, empty of food, with a son, ay, and a prophet.

Nor is it merely change of nature, or aversion of perils, or obliteration of sins, but likewise the recognition of mysteries, which fasts will merit from God. Look at Daniel's example. About the dream of the King of Babylon all the sophists are troubled: they affirm that, without external aid, it cannot be discovered by human skill. Daniel alone, trusting to God, and knowing what would tend to the deserving of God's favor, requires a space of three days, fasts with his fraternity, and—his prayers thus commended—is instructed throughout as to the order and signification of the dream; quarter is granted to the tyrant's sophists; God is glorified; Daniel is honored; destined as he was to receive, even subsequently also, no less a favor of God in the first year, of King Darius, when, after careful and repeated meditation upon the times predicted by

Jeremiah, he set his face to God in fasts, and sackcloth, and ashes. For the angel, withal, sent to him, immediately professed this to be the cause of the Divine approbation: "I am come," he said, "to demonstrate to thee, since thou art pitiable"—by fasting, to wit. If to God he was "pitiable," to the lions in the den he was formidable, where, six days fasting, he had breakfast provided him by an angel.

Chapter VIII. —Examples of a Similar Kind from the New.

We produce, too, our remaining (evidences). For we now hasten to modern proofs. On the threshold of the Gospel, Anna the prophetess, daughter of Phanuel, "who both recognized the infant Lord, and preached many things about Him to such as were expecting the redemption of Israel," after the pre-eminent distinction of long-continued and single husbanded widowhood, is additionally graced with the testimony of "fastings" also; pointing out, as she does, what the duties are which should characterize attendants of the Church, and (pointing out, too, the fact) that Christ is understood by none more than by the once married and often fasting.

By and by the Lord Himself consecrated His own baptism (and, in His own, that of all) by fasts; having (the power) to make "loaves out of stones," say, to make Jordan flow with wine perchance, if He had been such a "glutton and toper." Nay, rather, by the virtue of contemning food He was initiating "the new man" into "a severe handling" of "the old," that He might show that (new man) to the devil, again seeking to tempt him by means of *food*, (to be) too strong for the whole power of hunger.

Thereafter He prescribed to fasts a law—that they are to be performed "without sadness:" for why should what is salutary be sad? He taught likewise that fasts are to be the weapons for battling with the more direful demons: for what wonder if the same operation is the instrument of the iniquitous spirit's egress as of the Holy Spirit's ingress? Finally, granting that upon the centurion Cornelius, even *before baptism*, the honorable gift of the Holy Spirit, together with the gift of prophecy besides, had hastened to descend, we see that *his fasts* had been heard, I think, moreover, that the apostle too, in the Second of Corinthians, among his labors, and perils, and hardships, after "hunger and thirst," enumerates "fasts" also "very many."

Chapter IX. —From Fasts Absolute Tertullian Comes to Partial Ones and Xerophagies.

This principal species in the category of dietary restriction may already afford a prejudgment concerning the inferior operations of abstinence also, as being themselves too, in proportion to their measure, useful or necessary. For the exception of certain kinds from use of food is a partial fast. Let us therefore look into the question of the novelty or vanity of xerophagies, to see whether in them too we do not find an operation alike of most ancient as of most efficacious religion. I return to Daniel and his brethren, preferring as they did a diet of vegetables and the beverage of water to the royal dishes and decanters, and being found as they were therefore "more handsome" (lest any be apprehensive on the score of his paltry body, to boot!), besides being spiritually cultured into the bargain. For God gave to the young men knowledge and understanding in every kind of literature, and to Daniel in every word, and in dreams, and in every kind of wisdom; which (wisdom) was to make him wise in this very thing also, —namely, by what means the recognition of mysteries was to be obtained from God. Finally, in the third year of Cyrus king of the Persians, when he had fallen into careful and repeated meditation on a vision, he provided another form of humiliation. "In those days," he says, "I Daniel was mourning during three weeks: pleasant bread I ate not; flesh and wine entered not into my mouth; with oil I was not anointed; until three weeks were consummated:" which being elapsed, an angel was sent out (from God), addressing him on this wise: "Daniel, thou art a man pitiable; fear not: since, from the first day on which thou gravest thy soul to recogitation and to humiliation before God, thy word hath been heard, and I am entered at thy word." Thus the "pitiable" spectacle and the humiliation of xerophagies expel fear, and attract the ears of God, and make men masters of secrets.

I return likewise to Elijah. When the ravens had been wont to satisfy him with "bread and *flesh*," why was it that afterwards, at Beersheba of Judea, that certain angel, after rousing him from sleep, offered him, beyond doubt, bread *alone*, and water? Had ravens been wanting, to feed him more liberally? or had it been difficult to the "angel" to carry away from some pan of the banquet-room of the king some attendant with his amply-furnished waiter, and transfer him to Elijah, just as the breakfast of the reapers was carried into the den of lions and presented to Daniel in his hunger? But it behooved that an example should be set, teaching us that, at a time of pressure and persecution and whatsoever difficulty, we must live on xerophagies. With such food did David express his own exomologesis; "eating ashes indeed as it were bread," that is, bread dry and foul like ashes: "mingling, moreover, his drink with weeping"—of course, instead of wine. For *abstinence from wine* withal has honorable badges of its own: (an abstinence) which had dedicated Samuel, and consecrated Aaron, to God. For of Samuel his mother said: "And wine and that which is intoxicating shall he not drink:" for such was her condition withal when praying to God. And the Lord said to Aaron: "Wine and spirituous liquor shall ye not drink, thou and thy son after thee, whenever ye shall enter the tabernacle, or ascend unto the sacrificial altar; and ye shall not die." So true is it, that such as shall have ministered in the Church, being not sober, shall "die." Thus, too, in recent times He upbraids Israel: "And ye used to give my sanctified ones wine to drink." And, moreover, this limitation upon drink is the portion of xerophagy. Anyhow, wherever abstinence from wine is either exacted by God or vowed by man, there let there be understood likewise a restriction of *food* fore-furnishing a formal type to *drink*. For the quality of the drink is correspondent to that of the eating. It is not probable that a man should sacrifice to God *half* his appetite; temperate in waters, and intemperate in meats. Whether, moreover, the apostle had any acquaintance with xerophagies— (the apostle) who had repeatedly practiced greater rigors, "hunger, and thirst, and fasts many," who had forbidden "drunkennesses and reveling"—we have a sufficient evidence even from the case of his disciple Timotheus; whom when he admonishes, "for the sake of his stomach and constant weaknesses," to use "a little wine," from which he was abstaining not from rule, but from devotion—else the custom would rather have been beneficial to his stomach—by this very fact he has advised abstinence from wine as "worthy of God," which, on a ground of *necessity*, he has dissuaded.

Chapter X.—Of Stations, and of the Hours of Prayer.

In like manner they censure on the count of novelty our Stations as being *enjoined*; some, moreover, (censure them) too as being prolonged habitually too late, saying that this duty also ought to be observed of free choice, and not continued beyond the ninth hour, — (deriving their rule), of course, from their own practice. Well: as to that which pertains to the question of *injunction*, I will once for all give a reply to suit all causes. Now, (turning) to the point which is proper to this particular cause—concerning the limit of time, I mean—I must first demand from themselves whence they derive this prescriptive law for concluding Stations at the ninth hour. If it is from the fact that we read that Peter and he who was with him entered the temple "at the ninth (hour), the hour of prayer," who will prove to me that they had that day been performing a Station, so as to interpret the ninth hour as the hour for the conclusion and discharge of the Station? Nay, but you would more easily find that Peter at the *sixth* hour had, for the sake of taking food, gone up first on the roof to pray; so that the *sixth* hour of the day may the rather be made the limit to this duty, which (in Peter's case) was apparently to finish that duty, after prayer. Further: since in the self-same commentary of Luke the *third* hour is demonstrated as an hour of prayer, about which hour it was that they who had received the initiatory gift of the Holy Spirit were held for drunkards; and the *sixth*, at which Peter went up on the roof; and the *ninth*, at which they entered the temple: why should we not understand that, with absolutely perfect indifference, we must pray always, and everywhere, and at every time; yet still that these three hours, as being more marked in things human—(hours) which divide the day, which distinguish businesses, which re-echo in the public ear—have likewise ever been of special solemnity in divine prayers? A persuasion which is sanctioned also by the corroborative fact of Daniel praying thrice in the day; of course, through exception of certain stated hours, no other, moreover, than the more marked and subsequently apostolic (hours)—the third, the sixth, the ninth. And hence, accordingly, I shall affirm that Peter too had been led rather by ancient usage to the observance of the ninth hour, praying at the third specific interval, (the interval) of final prayer.

These (arguments), moreover, (we have advanced) for their sakes who think that they are acting in conformity with Peter's model, (a model) of which they are ignorant: not as if we slighted the ninth hour, (an hour) which, on the fourth and sixth days of the week, we most highly honor; but because, of those things which are observed on the ground of tradition, we are bound to adduce so much the worthier reason, that they lack the authority of Scripture, until by some signal celestial gift they be either confirmed or else corrected.

"And if," says (the apostle), "there are matters which ye are ignorant about, the Lord will reveal to you." Accordingly, setting out of the question the confirmer of all such things, the

Paraclete, the guide of universal truth, inquire whether there be not a worthier reason adduced among *us* for the observing of the ninth hour; so that this reason (of ours) must be attributed even to Peter if he observed a Station at the time in question. For (the practice) comes from the death of the Lord; which death albeit it behooves to be commemorated always, without difference of hours; yet are we at that time more impressively commended to its commemoration, according to the actual (meaning of the) name of Station. For even soldiers, though never unmindful of their military oath, yet pay a greater deference to Stations. And so the "pressure" must be maintained up to that hour in which the orb—involved from the sixth hour in a general darkness—performed for its dead Lord a sorrowful act of duty; so that we too may then return to enjoyment when the universe regained its sunshine. If this savors more of the spirit of Christian religion, while it celebrates more the glory of Christ, I am equally able, from the self-same order of events, to fix the condition of *late protraction of the Station*; (namely), that we are to fast till a late hour, awaiting the time of the Lord's sepulture, when Joseph took down and entombed the body which he had requested. Thence (it follows) that it is even irreligious for the flesh of the servants to take refreshment before their Lord did.

But let it suffice to have thus far joined issue on the *argumentative* challenge; rebutting, as I have done, conjectures by conjectures, and yet (as I think) by conjectures more worthy of a believer. Let us see whether any such (principle) drawn from the ancient times takes us under its patronage.

In Exodus, was not that position of Moses, battling against Amalek by prayers, maintained as it was perseveringly even till "sunset," a "late Station?" Think we that Joshua the son of Nun, when warring down the Amorites, had breakfasted on that day on which he ordered the very elements to keep a Station? The sun "stood" in Gibeon, and the moon in Ajalon; the sun and the moon "stood in station until the People was avenged of his enemies, and the sun stood in the mid heaven." When, moreover, (the sun) did draw toward his setting and the end of the one day, there was no such day before time and in the latest time (of course, (no day) so *long*), "that God," says (the writer), "should hear a man"— (a man,) to be sure, the sun's peer, so long persistent in his duty—a Station longer even than *late*.

At all events, Saul himself, when engaged in battle, manifestly *enjoined* this duty: "Cursed (be) the man who shall have eaten bread until evening, until I avenge me on mine enemy;" and his whole people tasted not (food), and (yet) the whole earth was breakfasting! So solemn a sanction, moreover, did God confer on the edict which enjoined that Station, that Jonathan the son of Saul, although it had been in ignorance of the fast having been appointed till a late hour that he had allowed himself a taste of honey, was both presently convicted, by lot, of sin, and with difficulty exempted from punishment through the prayer of the People: for he had been convicted of gluttony, although of a simple kind. But withal Daniel, in the first year of King Darius, when, fasting in sackcloth and ashes, he was doing exomologesis to God, said: "And while I was still speaking in prayer, behold, the man whom I had seen in dreams at the beginning, swiftly flying, approached me, as it were, at the hour of the evening sacrifice." This will be a "late" Station which, fasting *until the evening*, sacrifices a fatter (victim of) prayer to God!

Chapter XI. —Of the Respect Due to "Human Authority;" And of the Charges of "Heresy" And "Pseudo-Prophecy."

But all these (instances) I believe to be unknown to those who are in a state of agitation at our proceedings; or else known by the reading alone, not by careful study as well; in accordance with the greater bulk of "the unskilled" among the over boastful multitude, to wit, of the Psychics. This is why we have steered our course straight through the different individual species of fastings, of xerophagies, of stations: in order that, while we recount, according to the materials which we find in either Testament, the advantages which the dutiful observances of abstinence from, or curtailment or deferment of, food confer, we may refute those who invalidate these things as empty observances; and again, while we similarly point out in what rank of religious duty they have always had place, may confute those who accuse them as novelties: for neither is that novel which has always been, nor that empty which is useful.

The question, however, still lies before us, that some of these observances, having been commanded by God to man, have constituted this practice legally binding; some, offered by man to God, have discharged some votive obligation. Still, even a vow, when it has been accepted by God, constitutes a law for the time to come, owing to the authority of the Acceptor; for he who has given his approbation to a deed, when done, has given a mandate for its doing thenceforward. And so from this consideration, again, the wrangling of the opposite party is silenced, while they say: "It is either a pseudo-prophecy, if it is a spiritual voice which institutes these your solemnities; or else a heresy, if it is a human presumption which devises them." For, while censuring that form in which the ancient economies ran their course, and at the same time drawing out of that form arguments to hurl back (upon us) which the very adversaries of the ancient economies will in their turn be able to retort, they will be bound either to reject those arguments, or else to undertake these proven duties (which they impugn): necessarily so; chiefly because these very duties (which they impugn), from whatsoever institutor they are, be he a spiritual man or merely an ordinary believer, direct their course to the honor of the same God as the ancient economies. For, indubitably, both heresy and pseudo-prophecy will, in the eyes of us who are all priests of one only God the Creator and of His Christ, be judged by diversity of divinity: and so far forth I defend this side indifferently, offering my opponents to join issue on whatever ground they choose. "It is the spirit of the devil," you say, O Psychic. And how is it that he enjoins duties which belong to our God, and enjoins them to be offered to none other than our God? Either contend that the devil works with our God, or else let the Paraclete be held to be Satan. But you affirm it is "a human Antichrist:" for by this name heretics are called in John. And how is it that, whoever he is, he has in (the name of) our Christ directed these duties toward our Lord; whereas withal antichrists have (ever) gone forth (professedly teaching) towards God, (but) in opposition to our Christ? On which side, then, do you think the Spirit is confirmed as existing among us; when He commands, or when He approves, what our God has always both commanded and approved? But you again set up boundary-posts to God, as with regard to grace, so with regard to discipline; as with regard to gifts, so, too, with regard to solemnities: so that our observances are supposed to have ceased in like manner as His benefits; and you thus deny that He still continues to impose duties, because, in this case again, "the Law and the prophets (were) until John." It remains for you to banish Him wholly, being, as He is, so far as lies in *you*, so otiose.

Chapter XII—Of the Need for Some Protest Against the Psychics and Their Self-Indulgence.

For, by this time, in this respect as well as others, "you are reigning in wealth and satiety"—not making inroads upon such sins as fasts diminish, nor feeling need of such revelations as xerophagies extort, nor apprehending such wars of your own as Stations dispel. Grant that from the time of John the Paraclete had grown mute; we ourselves would have arisen as prophets to ourselves, for this cause chiefly: I say not now to bring down by our prayers God's anger, nor to obtain his protection or grace; but to secure by premonition the moral position of the "latest times;" enjoining every species of ταπεινοφρόνησις, since the prison must be familiarized to us, and hunger and thirst practiced, and capacity of enduring as well the absence of food as anxiety about it acquired: in order that the Christian may enter into prison in like condition as if he had (just) come forth of it,—to suffer there not penalty, but discipline, and not the world's tortures, but his own habitual observances; and to go forth out of custody to (the final) conflict with all the more confidence, having nothing of sinful false care of the flesh about him, so that the tortures may not even have material to work on, since he is cuirassed in a mere dry skin, and cased in horn to meet the claws, the succulence of his blood already sent on (heavenward) before him, the baggage as it were of his soul,—the soul herself withal now hastening (after it), having already, by frequent fasting, gained a most intimate knowledge of death!

Plainly, *your* habit is to furnish cook shops in the prisons to untrustworthy martyrs, for fear they should miss their accustomed usages, grow weary of life, (and) be stumbled at the novel discipline of abstinence; (a discipline) which not even the well-known Pristinus—*your* martyr, no *Christian* martyr—had ever come in contact with: he whom—stuffed as he had long been, thanks to the facilities afforded by the "free custody" (now in vogue, and) under an obligation, I suppose, to all the baths (as if they were better than baptism!), and to all the retreats of voluptuousness (as if they were more secret than those of the Church!), and to all the allurements of this life (as if they were of more worth than those of life eternal!), not to be willing to die—on the very last day of trial, at high noon, you premedicated with drugged wine as an antidote, and so completely enervated, that on being tickled—for his intoxication made it feel like tickling—with a few claws, he was unable any more to make answer to the presiding officer interrogating him "whom he confessed to be Lord;" and, being now put on the rack for this silence, when he could utter nothing but hiccoughs and belchings, died in the very act of apostasy! This is why they who preach sobriety are "false prophets;" this why they who practice it are "heretics!" Why then hesitate to believe that the Paraclete, whom you deny in a Montanus, exists in an Apicius?

Chapter XIII. —Of the Inconsistencies of the Psychics.

You lay down a prescription that this faith has its solemnities "appointed" by the Scriptures or the tradition of the ancestors; and that no further addition in the way of observance must be added, on account of the unlawfulness of innovation. Stand on that ground, if you can. For, behold, I impeach you of fasting besides on the Paschal-day, beyond the limits of those days in which "the Bridegroom was taken away;" and interposing the half-fasts of Stations; and you, (I find), sometimes living on bread and water, when it has seemed meet to each (so to do). In short, you answer that "these things are to be done of choice, not of command." You have changed your ground, therefore, by exceeding tradition, in undertaking observances which have not been "appointed." But what kind of deed is it, to permit to your own choice what you grant not to the command of God? Shall human volition have more license than Divine power? I am mindful that I am free from *the world*, not from God. Thus it is my part to perform, without external suggestion thereto, an act of respect to my Lord, it is His to enjoin. I ought not merely to pay a willing obedience to Him, but withal to court Him; for the former I render to His command, the latter to my own choice.

But it is enough for me that it is a customary practice for the bishops withal to issue mandates for fasts to the universal commonalty of the Church; I do not mean for the special purpose of collecting contributions of alms, as your beggarly fashion has it, but sometimes too from some particular cause of ecclesiastical solicitude. And accordingly, if you practice ταπεινοφρόνησις at the bidding of a man's edict, and all unitedly, how is it that in our case you set a brand upon the very unity also of our fastings, and xerophagies, and

Stations? —unless, perhaps, it is against the decrees of the senate and the mandates of the emperors which are opposed to "meetings" that we are sinning! The Holy Spirit, when He was preaching in whatsoever lands He chose, and through whomsoever He chose, was wont, from foresight of the imminence either of temptations to befall the Church, or of plagues to befall the world, in His character of Paraclete (that is, Advocate for the purpose of winning over the judge by prayers), to issue mandates for observances of this nature; for instance, at the present time, with the view of practicing the discipline of sobriety and abstinence: we, who receive Him, must necessarily observe also the appointments which He then made. Look at the Jewish calendar, and you will find it nothing novel that all succeeding posterity guards with hereditary scrupulousness the precepts given to the fathers. Besides, throughout the provinces of Greece there are held in definite localities those councils gathered out of the universal Churches, by whose means not only all the deeper questions are handled for the common benefit, but the actual representation of the whole Christian name is celebrated with great veneration. (And how worthy a thing is this, that, under the auspices of faith, men should congregate from all quarters to Christ! "See, how good and how enjoyable for brethren to dwell in unity!" This psalm *you* know not easily how to sing, except when you are supping with a goodly company!) But those conclaves first, by the operations of Stations and fastings, know what it is "to grieve with the grieving," and thus at last "to rejoice in company with the rejoicing." If we also, in our diverse provinces, (but) present mutually in spirit, observe those very solemnities, whose then celebration our present discourse has been defending, that is the sacramental law.

Chapter XIV. —Reply to the Charge of "Galaticism."

Being, therefore, observers of "seasons" for these things, and of "days, and months, and years," we *Galaticize*.

Plainly we do, if we are observers of *Jewish* ceremonies, of *legal* solemnities: for *those* the apostle unteaches, suppressing the continuance of the Old Testament which has been buried in Christ, and establishing that of the New. But if there is a new creation in Christ, our solemnities too will be bound to be new: else, if the apostle has erased *all* devotion absolutely "of seasons, and days, and months, and years," why do we celebrate the Passover by an *annual* rotation in the *first month*? Why in the *fifty* ensuing *days* do we spend our time in all exultation? Why do we devote to Stations the *fourth* and *sixth* days of the week, and to fasts the "*preparation-day*?" Anyhow, *you* sometimes continue your Station even over the Sabbath, —a day never to be kept as a fast except at the Passover season, according to a reason elsewhere given. With us, at all events, *every* day likewise is celebrated by an ordinary consecration. And it will not, then, be, in the eyes of the apostle, the *differentiating principle*—distinguishing (as he is doing) "things new and old"—which will be ridiculous; but (in this case too) it will be your own unfairness, while you taunt us with the *form* of *antiquity* all the while you are laying against us the *charge* of *novelty*.

Chapter XV. —Of the Apostle's Language Concerning Food.

The apostle reprobates likewise such as "bid to abstain from meats; but he does so from the foresight of the Holy Spirit, precondemning already the heretics who would enjoin *perpetual* abstinence to the extent of destroying and despising the works of the Creator; such as I may find in the person of a Marcion, a Tatian, or a Jupiter, the Pythagorean heretic of to-day; not in the person of the Paraclete. For how limited is the extent of *our* "interdiction of meats!" Two weeks of xerophagies in the year (and not the whole of these, —the Sabbaths, to wit, and the Lord's days, being excepted) we offer to God; abstaining from things which we do not *reject*, but *defer*. But further: when writing to the Romans, the apostle now gives *you* a home-thrust, detractors as you are of this observance: "Do not for the sake of food," he says, "undo the work of God." What "work?" That about which he says, "It is good not to eat flesh, and not to drink wine:" "for he who in these points doeth service, is pleasing and propitiable to our God." "One believeth that all things may be eaten; but another, being weak, feedeth on vegetables. Let not him who eateth lightly esteem him who eateth not. Who art thou, who judgest another's servant?" "Both he who eateth, and he who eateth not, giveth God thanks." But, since he forbids *human* choice to be made matter of controversy, how much more *Divine*! Thus he knew how to chide certain restricters and interdicters of food, such as abstained from it of contempt, not of duty; but to approve such as did so to the honor, not the insult, of the Creator. And if he has "delivered you the keys of the meat-market," permitting the eating of "all things" with a view to establishing the exception of "things offered to idols;" still he has not included the kingdom of God in the meat-market: "For," he says, "the kingdom of God is neither meat nor drink;" and, "Food commendeth us not to God"—not that you may think this said about *dry* diet, but rather about rich and carefully prepared, if, when he subjoins, "Neither, if we shall have eaten, shall we abound; nor, if we shall not have eaten, shall we be deficient," the ring of his words suits, (as it does), you rather (than us), who think that you do "abound" if you eat, and are "deficient if you eat not; and for this reason disparage these observances.

How unworthy, also, is the way in which you interpret to the favor of your own lust the fact that the Lord "ate and drank" promiscuously! But I think that He must have likewise "fasted" inasmuch as He has pronounced, not "the full," but "the hungry and thirsty, blessed:" (He) who was wont to profess "food" to be, not that which His disciples had supposed, but "the thorough doing of the Father's work;" teaching "to labor for the meat which is permanent unto life eternal;" in our ordinary prayer likewise commanding us to request "bread," not the wealth of Attalus therewithal. Thus, too, Isaiah has *not* denied that God "hath chosen" *a* "fast;" but has particularized in detail the *kind* of fast which He has *not* chosen: "for in the days," he says, "of your fasts your own wills are found (indulged), and all who are subject to you ye stealthily sting; or else ye fast with a view to abuse and strifes, and ye smite with the fists. Not *such* a fast have I elected;" but such a one as He has subjoined, and by subjoining has not abolished, but confirmed.

Chapter XVI. —Instances from Scripture of Divine Judgments Upon the Self-Indulgent; And Appeals to the Practices of Heathens.

For even if He does *prefer* "the works of righteousness," still not without a sacrifice, which is a soul afflicted with fasts. He, at all events, is the God to whom neither a People incontinent of appetite, nor a priest, nor a prophet, was pleasing. To this day the "monuments of concupiscence" remain, where the People, greedy of "flesh," till, by devouring without digesting the quails, they brought on cholera, were buried. Eli breaks his neck before the temple doors, his sons fall in battle, his daughter-in-law expires in child-birth: for such was the blow which had been deserved at the hand of God by the shameless house, the defrauder of the fleshly sacrifices. Sameas, a "man of God," after prophesying the issue of the idolatry introduced by King Jeroboam—after the drying up and immediate restoration of that king's hand—after the rending in twain of the sacrificial altar,—being on account of these signs invited (home) by the king by way of recompense, plainly declined (for he had been prohibited by God) to touch food at all in that place; but having presently afterwards rashly taken food from another old man, who lyingly professed himself a prophet, he was deprived, in accordance with the word of God then and there uttered over the table, of burial in his fathers' sepulchers. For he was prostrated by the rushing of a lion upon him in the way, and was buried among strangers; and thus paid the penalty of his breach of fast.

These will be warnings both to people and to bishops, even spiritual ones, in case they may ever have been guilty of incontinence of appetite. Nay, even in Hades the admonition has not ceased to speak; where we find in the person of the rich feaster, convivialities tortured; in that of the pauper, fasts refreshed; having— (as convivialities and fasts alike had)—as preceptors "Moses and the prophets." For Joel withal exclaimed: "Sanctify a fast, and a religious service;" foreseeing even then that other apostles and prophets would sanction fasts, and would preach observances of special service to God. Whence it is that even they who court their *idols* by dressing them, and by adorning them in their sanctuary, and by saluting them at each particular hour, are said to do them *service*. But, more than that, the heathens recognize every form of ταπεινοφρόνησις. When the heaven is rigid and the year arid, barefooted processions are enjoined by public proclamation; the magistrates lay aside their purple, reverse the fasces, utter prayer, offer a victim. There are, moreover, some colonies where, besides (these extraordinary solemnities, the inhabitants), by an annual rite, clad in sackcloth and besprent with ashes, present a suppliant importunity to their idols, (while) baths and shops are kept shut till the ninth hour. They have one single fire in public— on the altars; no water even in their platters. There is, I believe, a Ninevitan suspension of business! A Jewish fast, at all events, is universally celebrated; while, neglecting the temples, throughout all the shore, in every open place, they continue long to send prayer up to heaven. And, albeit by the dress and ornamentation of mourning they disgrace the duty, still they do affect a faith in abstinence, and sigh for the arrival of the long-lingering

evening star to sanction (their feeding). But it is enough for me that you, by heaping blasphemies upon *our* xerophagies, put them on a level with the chastity of an Isis and a Cybele.
I admit the comparison in the way of evidence. Hence (our xerophagy) will be proved divine, which the devil, the emulator of things divine, imitates. It is out of truth that falsehood is built; out of religion that superstition is compacted. Hence *you* are more irreligious, in proportion as a heathen is more conformable. He, in short, sacrifices his appetite to an idol god; *you* to (the true) God will not. For to you your belly is god, and your lungs a temple, and your paunch a sacrificial altar, and your cook the priest, and your fragrant smell the Holy Spirit, and your condiments spiritual gifts, and your belching prophecy.

Chapter XVII. —Conclusion.

"Old" you are, if we will say the truth, you who are so indulgent to appetite, and justly do you vaunt your "priority:" always do I recognize the savor of Esau, the hunter of wild beasts: so unlimitedly studious are you of catching fieldfares, so do you come from "the field" of your most lax discipline, so faint are you in spirit. If I offer you a paltry lentil dyed red with must well boiled down, forthwith you will sell all your "primacies:" with you "love" shows its fervor in sauce-pans, "faith" its warmth in kitchens, "hope" its anchorage in waiters; but of greater account is "love," because that is the means whereby your young men sleep with their sisters! Appendages, as we all know, of appetite are lasciviousness and voluptuousness. Which alliance the apostle withal was aware of; and hence, after premising, "Not in drunkenness and revels," he adjoined, "nor in couches and lusts."

To the indictment of your appetite pertains (the charge) that "double honor" is with you assigned to your presiding (elders) by double shares (of meat and drink); whereas the apostle has given them "double honor" as being both *brethren* and *officers*. Who, among you, is superior in holiness, except him who is more frequent in banqueting, more sumptuous in catering, more learned in cups? Men of soul and flesh alone as you are, justly do you reject things spiritual. If the prophets were pleasing to *such*, my (prophets) they were not. Why, then, do not you constantly preach, "Let us eat and drink, for to-morrow we shall die?" just as *we* do not hesitate manfully to command, "Let us fast, brethren and sisters, lest to-morrow perchance we die." Openly let us vindicate our disciplines. Sure we are that "they who are in the flesh cannot please God;" not, of course, those who are in the *substance* of the flesh, but in the *care*, the *affection*, the *work*, the *will*, of it. Emaciation displeases not us; for it is not by weight that God bestows flesh, any more than He does "the Spirit by measure." More easily, it may be, through the "strait gate" of salvation will slenderer flesh enter; more speedily will lighter flesh rise; longer in the sepulcher will drier flesh retain its firmness. Let Olympic cestus-players and boxers cram themselves to satiety. To them bodily ambition is suitable to whom bodily strength is necessary; and yet they also strengthen themselves by xerophagies. But ours are other thews and other sinews, just as our contests withal are other; we whose "wrestling is not against flesh and blood, but against the world's power, against the spiritualties of malice." Against these it is not by robustness of flesh and blood, but of faith and spirit, that it behooves us to make our antagonistic stand. On the other hand, an over-fed Christian will be more necessary to bears and lions, perchance, than to God; only that, even to encounter beasts, it will be his duty to practice emaciation.

Elucidations.

I.

(Greater license, p. 104.)

In this treatise, which is designed to justify the extremes of Montanistic fasts, Tertullian's genius often surprises us by his ingenuity. This is one of the instances where the forensic orator comes out, trying to outflank and turn the position of an antagonist who has gained an advantage. The fallacy is obvious. Kaye cites, in comparison, a passage from "The Apparel of Women," and another from "The Exhortation to Chastity." He remarks, "Were we required to produce an instance [i.e. to prove the tendency of mankind to run into extremes], we should without hesitation refer the reader to this treatise."

Fasting was ordained of Christ Himself as a means to an end. It is here reduced from its instrumental character, and made an excuse for dividing the household of faith, and for cruel accusations against brethren.

In our age of an entire relaxation of discipline, the enthusiast may nevertheless awaken us, perhaps, to honest self-examination as to our manner of life, in view of the example of Christ and His apostles, and their holy precepts.

II.

(Provinces of Greece, p. 111.)

We have here an interesting hint as to the ἀρχαῖα ἔθη to which the Council of Nice refers in one of her most important canons. Provinces, synods, and the charges or pastoral letters of the bishops are referred to as established institutions. And note the emphasis given to "Greece" as the mother of churches, and of laws and customs. He looks Eastward, and not by any means to the West, for high examples of the Catholic usages by which he was endeavoring to justify his own.

III.

(An over-fed Christian, p. 114.)

"Are we not carnal" (psychics) in our days? May not the very excesses of Tertullian sting and reproach us with the charge of excessive indulgence (Matt. ix. 15)? The "over-fed Christians" whom he here reproaches are proved by this very treatise to have observed a system of fasting which is little practiced anywhere in our times—for a mere change to luxurious fish-diet is the very mockery of fasting. We learn that the customary fasts of these *psychics* were as follows: (1) the annual Paschal fast, from Friday till Easter-Day; (2) Wednesdays and Fridays (stationary days) every week; and (3) the "dry-food days,"—abstinence from "pleasant bread" (Dan. x. 2),—though some Catholics objected to these voluntary abstinences.

IV.

(Practice emaciation, p. 114.)

Think of our Master's fast among the wild beasts! Let us condescend to go back to Clement, to Origen, and to Tertullian to learn the practical laws of the Gospel against avarice, luxury, and "the deceitfulness of sin." I am emboldened to say this by some remarkable words which I find, to my surprise, thrown out *in a scientific work* proceeding from Harvard University. It is with exceeding gratitude that I quote as follows: "*It is well to go away at times, that we may see another aspect of human life* which still survives in the East, and to feel that influence which led even the Christ into the wilderness to prepare for the struggle with the animal nature of man. We need something of the experience of the Anchorites of Egypt, to impress us with the great truth that the distinction between the spiritual and the material remains broad and clear, even if with the scalpel of our modern philosophy we cannot completely dissect the two; and this experience will give us courage to cherish our aspirations, keep bright our hopes, and hold fast our Christian faith until the consummation comes."

www.ingramcontent.com/pod-product-compliance
Lightning Source LLC
Chambersburg PA
CBHW071014120726
47910CB00004B/1523

* 9 7 8 1 6 4 3 7 3 0 8 7 5 *